T0132287

Requited Love

A Search

ROBERT ROGERS

To order additional copies of this book, contact:
Xlibris
844-714-8691
www.Xlibris.com
Orders@Xlibris.com

ISBN: 978-1-6641-4089-9 (sc)
ISBN: 978-1-6641-4088-2 (e)

Print information available on the last page

Rev. date: 11/10/2020

Acknowledgements

I cannot name anyone who helped me
write these poems
I only have myself to blame

Contents

Change Your Mind

You may change your mind
But will your heart follow?
Forget me?
Drawn to what you see?

True love is hard to find
Will it be like mine
You have known her a short time
Will she love you

Women can be different than men
They flirt
Not meaning to cause heart
Just enjoy what they do

It's an interesting game
Not love
Not the same
Not remain

Come to me
Show you what love can be
Hold me
Laugh with me

I want you
Know how I feel
My love is real
Make love to me
I know what you like
So do I
Let us be together
Share a life

1

Discover Love

I haven't done this before
I am not sure what to do
Do you?
We can learn together

Where should we go
I don't know
Let's walk

Do you love me?
I'm new to this
As far as we have gone is to kiss
I hope love is like this
Bliss

We will learn
You are a woman and I'm a man
Both may discover love
I hope we can

Let's walk slow
Not rush
Be sure we want to do this
Maybe just kiss

When will we know?
I do want you so
Making love will be new
Beyond kissing you
Let's try

Love making taught us a lot
We now know
It's well beyond a kiss
True bliss

Is this lasting love?
I think it is
We need to learn again
Have it last
It will not be the first

Feelings I dream of

We once had something
Fleeing's I still dream of
A closeness that was exciting
A love we did not hide

What went wrong?
A disappointing song
The music died
The words I still remember
Burning memories

I love you
I want you
Hold me
Let me be with you
Take me

What a joyful time
The lyrics no longer rhyme
They are hidden
We sing alone

I remember that dress you wore
I see it in my dream
An imagination It seems
Will I ever see it again?

I want to see it drop to the floor
See you close the door
Walk to me
Love me

I wake and feel the pain
I want to hold you again
Know that love
Jointly sing that loving song
What went wrong?

He is not worth you

He is not worth you
He doesn't have a loving touch

He likes others
Often stays with them
Has sexual encounters
He is not worth you

Shed him and stay with me
It's an earnest plea
I will love you like no-one can
Heed my pleading stand

We will watch Miss Flower's Mysteries
Be entranced
See you change your hair
I can provide the rest

For a loving reality
Join me
He is not worth you

We will love each other
Dance in the living room
Just give me a change
See what tomorrow brings

I'll play a record
Linda Ronstadt's Desperado
I feel the love when you are around
Dance with me
He is not worth you
I treasure you

Help Me

Help Me
Share your love with me
Loving I like
But It must be right

I love you
Love me
Hold me tight
Resolve this longing plight

Cool this fire
Fill my desire
You are what I require
Help me

Be a loving man
Hold this hand
Follow me
Smile

We will linger for awhile
Touch
Not rush
Haste has few rewards

Caress me
Strum
Listen to the sound
Music will abound

I know you
I want you with me
I will show you
Don't refuse

You will know in time
This love of mine
I need you
Help me

I Dream Her

Once she was clearly mine
Now I'm here alone
Will my love be real?
I'm the only one who knows

I dream and see her
She is still mine
My dream is growing cold
She I no longer can hold

I don't know what is wrong
It's like an unknown song
The lyrics linger on
The music is gone

I once held her in my arms
I don't know if my dream will come true
I'm the only one who will know
It troubles me so

When I sleep I find her
Hold her in my arms
I don't know why the love is becoming cold
She is still mine

When I'm awake
I search to find her
My dream may come true
I'm the only one who will know

Some day
We may sleep and dream together

I Know

Your love is sweet
But not complete
You try not to let it show
I do know

Your touch is restrained
That gentle caress does not remain
It bothers me
I love that wanting touch

Tell me what you feel
Help me
I love you so much
Gently touch me again

Let me feel that warming embrace
Relight the fire
Let it burn in both our hearts
Remember how it feels
Make it real

Why have you changed?
Something I did?
Did not do?
Tell me

Let me touch you
Show me what to do
How to fully love you
Will I feel your tenderness again?
I want too

I Want to Love You

I want to love you
You won't let me
I don't know why
Was it something I said?
I need to know

You walked away
I didn't know what to say
I'll be alright
Vanity plays its part

I need to change my life
Learn what true love is like
I don't learn well
What the Hell!

I want to see you again
It's just the way I feel
I don't know why
I'd give my life to see you again

Fulfill my quest
Get past this vainness
Tell me what to do
How to love you

What must I do?
Open that love book
Read to me
Help me learn

I'm Older Now

I want to talk to you
You are the only one I have ever cared for
Time and my love have changed me
Talk to me

I believe in you
Please believe in me
Mend this broken heart
Give me a new start

I hope she knows
I loved her so
My life has moved at a rapid pace

I look at my life and wonder
What would I change?
A lot of things

I wouldn't drink that much
Neglect that woman's touch
Showed a little class
Made love last

I should have smiled and kissed her
Held her tight
Made things right
I no longer know how to rhyme
I should change the words

I've made a lot of mistakes
When will my poems die?
It will be a silent cry
My life shall soon surrender
Hope she remembers when my poems died

I wonder how she will feel
I hope she knows I loved her so

Let Me love You

I Want you
Long to be with you
Touch you
Let me love you

I know you want me
You told me so
Come close
Put a hand on my heart
Let that be a start

Touch the warmth
Feel the heart
It beats faster
I love your touch

Tell me what you feel
Let me see the glow in your eyes
Watch you brush your hair back
Gently put your lips to mine

I do want you
Let me love you
Help me slow this beating heart
Hold you close

Our love is not a gamble
We both shall win
The love will remain
We are one

Let Us Go Back

Let us go back
Remember where we were
You loved me
We relished the night
Held each other tight

Forget those pajamas
Remember what you said
Love is bare
It cannot hide

Let us share
Remember
Know it is right
Love the night

We were young
Older now
Our love can be new
I do love you

I see that smile
You remember
Let us go back
Embrace that feeling

We cannot forget
Love cannot hide
Let us relight the flame
Rekindle
Glow

Love cannot hide
Forget those pajamas

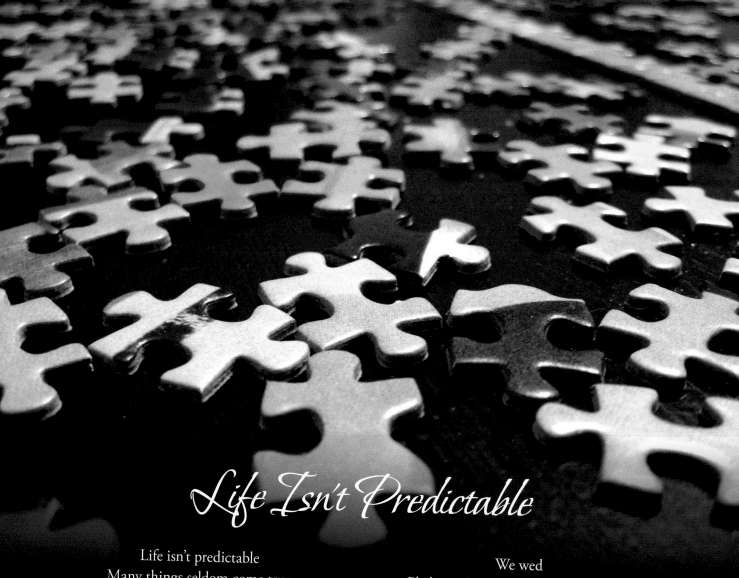

Life Isn't Predictable

Life isn't predictable
Many things seldom come true
Deciding what my child will be is not up to me
Must wait and see

Logic is according to the rules
Who can name them?
Not even in the schools where logic is sought
Predictions are at fault

The kids show up for school in pajamas
They may want to sleep
Geography makes them weep
When will they learn?
Never
What happens to unwritten rules?

Women will not wear those high heeled shoes
Nor put on that dress
Our standards change

We wed
Pledge to love each other until we die
That may not be true
We decide what not to do
Lasting love can be a guess
It's as changeable as all the rest

We search for the life we want to live
Work hard to succeed
We often concede
We don't remain the same

We wish the world were a peaceful place
It progresses at a frightening pace
Everything changes
Rules no longer remain

Life travels unknown paths
It doesn't last
Change will be forever
There is only one lasting exception

Lightning Strikes

Lightning strikes
Oh, how I love you
Sparks fly
I feel the fire

It ignites my heart
I held my hands to my breast
I waited for a cooling rain
The heat remained

When you touch me
My eyes brighten
I feel that fire
Love flares

I longer for the strike
I will know what love is like
It thunders in my breast
My mind follows

Your touch is a burning light
Makes my love burn bright
It feels right
Touch me again

Lightning begins in heaven
It brightens the sky
Thunder follows
Echo's in my heart

The touch comes from your hands
Heats me
I may never feel a cooling rain
I hope the fire remains

Love Again

Love again
I may not be the one
You may find another
Lose you forever

Will our love recover
Or just die forever
Can it stay alive?
Somehow survive
Decide

Look deep in your heart
Feel tomorrow
Will there be joy or sorrow
Take your time
Know you are right

Perhaps choose another
Know what your lifetime will contain
Life will not be the same
Bring light or darkness into your eyes
Sadness or laughter

Capturing long-lasting love is a choice
It's difficult
But It has exciting worth
Choose with care

I hope you choose me
Let me bring laughter
Eyes that glow
Then you will know
Exciting worth

Love no Longer Lasts

Don't come back
Leave me alone
You are not welcome
I will lock the door

Our love is gone
It no longer lasts
Strike me again?
My caring has past

Just walk away
I will not listen to what your say
I cannot live this way
Go away

I cannot love you anymore
You must know why'
Striking me was a sin
I will not let that happen again

Go find someone new
She may like you
I do not

You will never strike me again
A new life will begin
Live without the hurt

I'll sit on the porch
feel the sun
Know you are gone
Stop crying

My life will be new
Realize what I can do
Live without you
I smile

I'll watch the stars
Never again feel the pain
Know you will never hurt me again

Men Like Me

I'm getting older
Men seem to like me
I'm not sure what they see
Older women know what loving can be

I don't search for them
They come to me
As I walk along the sidewalk
They smile and walk beside me

We talk
They want to touch me
Hold my hand
I smile and tell them no

How far should I go
Do not know
Should tell them so?
They may not listen

They mean no harm
I do not know what they see
They just like me
I willingly walk with them

Maybe I should change this dress
It's just a guess
I wear what I like
Stroll the sidewalk
Talk to a man

I may let one hold my hand
Touch my dress
Fulfill my guess
I like getting older

Mend My Heart

Will you mend my heart?
Search for what you can find
Something broken
The thrill is gone

Love is not with me
It should be
You are no longer the loving kind
I know not what is on our mind

You may no longer love me
I do wish you could
Be loving
You are not mine

My heart may not mend
Please see what you can find
Try

Don' let me be alone
Our love may no longer meet
Love can be sweet
Taste

Come back to me
Just for a little while
Help mend this heart
Try

We both can change
Mend our lives
Love each other

Were Alone

When I awake in this bed
I remember what you said
I know what we had
Our love has changed

Our talk is grave
Neglect how we once behaved
You watch TV until I'm asleep
Silently come to bed

Making love is a task
It will not last
Lost that passion
A disquieting reaction

We no longer search for answers
Move in separate ways
Quietly walk through the days
There seems to be no new start

We accept how things are
Changed from lovers to silent friends
We're not sure how this will end
Perhaps drift further apart
Sleep in single beds

What about the kids?
Do they understand?
We stay together just to hold their hands
Keep them from crying

Life is strange
We always think love will remain
It can fall apart
Scatter from our hearts

You Lied

You lied to me
You said you loved me
I cannot mend this heart
I don't know where to start

I feel guilty
Tears run down my face
It's hard to let go
I did love you so

You don't love me
You closed the door
Never open it again
My tears will not fade

You wanted more
I tried
You said things were right
You lied

I should have known
Searched for the truth
Love is uncertain
It lives in an unknown place

Can You walk away
Start a new life
I wonder
Lies Last forever

I will always remember
You closed the door
I did so love you
I tried

You said you loved me
You lied

You Never Learn

Don't come home wild as can be
I'm not sure you love me
Some fools never learn
That could be me

Do not open the door
Walk into the house
Think nothing is wrong
You never learn

I try to say never
Your wildness may remain forever
Why do I love you?
Only God knows

You drink with your friends
Stagger through the door

Open me a beer
Maybe we can be the same

That wildness may enter me
After a couple of beers
We shall see
You won't be able to make love to me

I may never learn
Just watch you come home
Open that door
See you once more

Next time
Sit on the porch
Drink the beer in your hand
Forget making love to me
You can't

Making caring love requires soberness
You fail

Printed in the United States
By Bookmasters